Teacher Talk:
A Story Collection

Teacher Talk: A Story Collection

ADD YOUR STORY

Z Proudlock

Add Your Story to the website
http://teachertalkastorycollection-addyourstory.com

Facebook:
Teacher Talk: A Story Collection

ISBN: 1974429903
ISBN 13: 9781974429905
Library of Congress Control Number: 2017915931
CreateSpace Independent Publishing Platform
North Charleston, South Carolina

List of Contributors

Stephanie Alexander
Rosemary Armstrong
Donna Carson Ashukian
Deirdre Bennison
Paul Carter
Gail Davidson
Brian J. Harrison
Peter Lowens
Duncan McCallum
Pat Mooney
Zlata Proudlock
Anonymous

Cover Illustration by Rebecca Proudlock

*Dedicated to my husband, Michael; daughter,
Rebecca; and the contributors to this book.*

*Equally dedicated to my parents, members of the
Proudlock and Premrl families, and my friends.*

Acknowledgments

First and foremost, I want to thank my husband, Michael, and daughter, Rebecca, without whom this would not have been even possible. Michael edited the first drafts of this book with great patience, and he always had great suggestions for improvement. Rebecca graciously allowed me to illustrate this book with her original and truly beautiful art. This added a whole new dimension to the work and elevated the book to a higher level.

Most of all, I am forever grateful to the contributors of this book. To my dear friends and former colleagues, I am pleased to finally be able to say *thank you* and acknowledge all of you as champions of the teaching profession. You took a leap of faith by agreeing to take the time to respond to my e-mails in a thoughtful and intelligent manner. All these teachers are the most creative people I could possibly have encountered in many lifetimes. Their words allowed me to sew together this book— truly an integrated "yellow submarine" book if there ever was one! Without these gracious people, this book could not have been completed.

I want to thank the Peel District School Board, where I was fortunate to pursue most of my career. After thirty-seven years of teaching, it was the personal connections with students, teachers, secretarial staff, administrators, IT people, and custodial staff who made my job so much easier. I taught because I was supported by my department heads and was privileged to work closely with the awesome library teachers and coworkers in history, social science, and English when I was in the Yellow Submarine Office. I feel it is a great honor to have had the opportunity to be involved with so many wonderful people. Thanks also to my many friends and relatives who encouraged me through this process.

As well, I would like to thank all of my team at CreateSpace. Finally, thanks to Lisa Adams and Brian Henry, whose information helped me raise the level of each chapter.

I anticipated finishing this book much more quickly than four years after my retirement. The project morphed a bit from its original form, and life got in the way. But now it's done. Thank you all from the bottom of my heart. You are awesome.

—Zlata Proudlock

Contents

CHAPTER 1

Becoming a Teacher

When I was a student, I had a recurring nightmare that I had to run to school in my pajamas to make it to an exam. It was always the dead of winter, and I wore the grungiest pajamas ever!

This nightmare tormented me after I finished university. Apparently, it relates to a common fear of missing a test or failing in general. We all want to succeed, and we all have the common experience of being in school, taking tests, and knowing our teachers.

So, why is it some people say, "I'd never want to become a teacher!" while others can hardly wait to get back into the school system and work with young people? This chapter will offer some answers to this age-old question.

—ZP

And now, here are anecdotes and stories from the teachers who contributed to this book.

———

I decided to be a teacher on the first day of school in grade one. (No, we did not have kindergarten in those days!) I could not imagine life without going to school!

———

As a young girl in Toronto, I always enjoyed pretending I was a teacher. This was the best indoor game that didn't require six hours of time. One day, I insisted on playing school when I was at a friend's house, and we had gone through a beautiful trunk of clothes playing dress-up. I had a twenties' flapper costume on, and we were wondering what to do next. My girlfriend said she wanted to fix up my hair. I wasn't keen on it, especially when she told me that her career plan was to become a hairdresser for dead people. To me, this was a bit creepy, so I said I wanted to become a teacher, and I would rather play school. We played school not only because I was afraid of the dead-people scenario but also because I was keenly interested in seeing what it was like to be a teacher. It was a bit dark in her basement too. From seeing my own teachers, it looked like teaching school was going to be really easy—explaining things, writing notes, and assigning lines like "I must not talk in class" for homework. That sounded perfect, since I liked talking a lot and often had lines to write for homework.

———

I decided to be a teacher because I always loved history and grew up in a town that had a strong sense of history and Canada's beginnings as a nation. I wanted to impart this wonderful sense of the past and how important it was to us now and in the future.

———

I was having too much fun partying, dancing, and swimming, and generally hanging out to want to do any serious study, so a two-year teachers' college sounded about right! I continued to party and have fun while I did in college. I had expected to be married and have a house with a white picket fence before too long! Of course, that didn't happen.

———

In the 1970s, when I was growing up, young women didn't aspire to every job. It was pretty much teacher, nurse, or secretary. I had never seen a woman principal or vice principal. It seems grossly unfair and limiting to people today, but that was the mind-set, and it took a lot of time to realize these limitations were bad for everyone.

Men were rarely in nursing, but teaching was already for both sexes. Still, high-school departments usually had their male and female subjects.

I first became aware of the job division and limits to our choices when I started looking for part-time jobs in my teens. I opened the help-wanted ads of the Toronto newspaper in the late sixties and saw pages headed "Men Wanted" and "Women Wanted." I wondered why women and men were assigned to different jobs. Equality—I immediately understood what women's liberationists wanted, but I didn't know the history and all the personal battles people went through behind the headlines of marches and bra burning. Thankfully, these brave people opened doors for everyone. It's hard to remember just how much discrimination existed and how accepted it was. It has been a real battle to have jobs open to both sexes, and young people may not realize it wasn't always so. It didn't just go away because it was the right thing to do.

Teaching looked like a pretty open and fair work environment. Of course, today most people realize the difficulties faced by the LGBTQ community and other groups like the elderly and handicapped. Many would be upset that there still is unfairness. Now we have more laws that provide recourse.

———

Playing school was what we did when my friends came over. No one ever objected. This was a great indoor game. Other games we played were usually outside and involved balls tossed in the air, hide-and-seek, and biking up and down the street. Playing teacher was reserved for the cold winter or rainy days.

———

Why become a teacher? Back in the early sixties, girls graduating from high school in the prairies of Manitoba had limited options: nurse, secretary, teacher, or wife.

Only a select few went to university for whatever reason. There was no guidance department at school, and most of us knew little or nothing about a university degree. I wanted to join the air force and fly, but everyone decided that was not a good idea. I was pushed into teaching as something to fall back on.

———————

Pretending to be at school was fun as a kid. When I was the teacher, I was very strict, but when we reversed roles, I became a "bad student" and asked to go to the bathroom. That's how I probably decided that it would be fun to work with people all day. I might even change some young lives, just like in the TV shows about teachers. I thought teaching high school would be a bit like that.

I found out it wasn't exactly like TV, and I learned in the school of hard knocks in real life as a teacher. Who knows how deflating it is to be teaching a fantastic (or so I thought) lesson, only to have a student raise a hand to pose a question? But, unbeknown to you, the question is *not* about the pyramids or how genes come to be inherited. The question is not about the lesson at hand but "Can I go to the *bathroom*?" It screams at you, the teacher, "This is not interesting; let me out of here!" As a young teacher, you get disappointed; as an older teacher, you learn to say "No questions" at this point. This is the best advice so that students who are rapt in attention are not disturbed by distracted others.

———————

I, like many of my friends at university, was unsure of my career path. I was pursuing a bachelor of arts degree, and the only certainty I had at the time was that I was not cut out for any kind of repetitive type of work. I'd also ruled out any career that involved mechanical activity—how things worked and why were a mystery for me.

I had always enjoyed being around people and was narrowing down my course selections at the University of Toronto toward the social sciences, especially geography. In my third and fourth years, I was very fortunate to have had a couple of excellent professors who further excited me about the subject of geography. A decision to go to a teachers' college seemed a logical idea, although I certainly didn't see it as a passion by any means.

My experience at teachers' college was quite ho-hum; the classwork seemed too theoretical and impractical, while the practice-teaching sessions were impersonal and quite unsatisfactory.

I'd invested in five years of postsecondary education and a lot of money, so it wasn't an option to quit without trying at least a year of "real" teaching. Though I had very good grades, 1973 was not a good year for finding a teaching job. I was fortunate to land a job at a Television station where I was responsible for evaluating new social-science programming. It was very interesting work, and I knew it would help on my resume.

My real luck was deciding six months later to take a job teaching English as a Second Language to adults at George Brown

College in downtown Toronto. It wasn't geography, but it was still teaching. I absolutely loved it. I discovered I had the ability to make a difference in students' lives. They were learning, and I knew I was finding that very rewarding. At that point, I was quite confident that a career in teaching was the path to follow.

———

I wanted to be a teacher because I loved English. How could anyone not want to spend her life pursuing what she loved? My father worked for forty-three years at a job he hated; every day, I saw a defeated man come home, eat his supper, and go to bed. That was not what I wanted to do with my life.

———

I have always worked in aquatics; my options in teaching came from teaching swimming lessons to small children who gave me a smile.

I also had the opportunity to explore coaching and training National Lifeguard Service lifeguards for competitions and certifications. That forged the desire to give back to those who had given me opportunities when I was younger. Despite a few setbacks along the way, it only made my resolve deeper; I started to gain the confidence and insight into teaching, which gave me my beginning and helped forge a career. After graduating from university and trying a few entry-level jobs, I applied to teachers' college, not thinking I would even be considered; the rest, as they say, is history.

I know the power of observation has always been a rudimentary focus of mine from my science background, and I took it one step further in watching human interactions and behaviors. This gave me a heads-up when teaching swimming and first aid and helped me craft my lessons to the learner and not the curriculum. One of my mentors always told us when instructing children, to break skills up into simple steps and repeat, repeat, and repeat. As well, she taught that we should always view teaching from the learners' point of view.

———

Why did I decide to be a teacher? This is hard to answer simply. My parents really stressed education. Both had to leave school early; those were hard times and war years. While they didn't specify a career for me, they made sure that we all finished high school, and they funded my first two years of university. There were eight of us, so you can imagine that this was a major accomplishment. Six of us have university degrees, and two have college diplomas, so I think that as the sixth child, I automatically assumed I would be going to university. When I was in high school, I used to substitute for elementary teachers who were away for less than a day. One of the other teachers came by, looked into the room, and said to me: "You look like a natural!" In the summers, I worked in a kids' camp. I was fated to spend my life behind a desk or in front of one. I have never been so glad.

———

I think I always knew I would be a teacher, but after graduating with an honors English and drama degree, I took a job as a recreation director in an upscale retirement home. Why? Maybe to prove I could.

After a year of working with seniors in varying stages of retirement, I realized I wanted to spend the rest of my working days with younger people, who still had so much life to live.

I became a high school teacher of English, drama, and later, library and information skills. I loved working with colleagues who shared similar interests and administrators who inspired professional growth and school community. I especially enjoyed the students, who asked great questions that taught me something every day and kept me young through all the years.

Although there were many moments, particularly in the busy library environment, when I wished for a career in which I had to deal with only one person at a time, I cannot imagine one that could have been more stimulating, rewarding, or fulfilling overall than teaching.

———

I admired my phys. ed. teachers, who were more than willing to give up their time to coach and push us to our potential. Ron was the wrestling coach, and my phys. ed. teacher, who always said, "Be the best you can be."

———

I don't really know why I decided to become a teacher. My own school experience was not great; maybe I wanted to correct what I saw as problems in the system.

———

I loved learning how to write in cursive. The instruction in cursive was very elegant and unlike the staccato printing of words. Instead of a pencil, we got to use a pen—so much like art! How I loved to make the circles to practice staying between the lines—so round and luscious was each letter, rather than square and hard. I was thrilled and felt almost grown, because soon after, we learned how to write and sign a check! I felt this was *real* learning and I wanted in on it by becoming a teacher to reach other young people.

———

I decided to become a teacher because of past experiences teaching and coaching people in various organizations and capacities. I enjoyed these experiences and discovered that I liked teaching and had a knack for it.

———

I trust the stories you have just read in this chapter have jogged some memories and given you a starting point for your own reminiscences. There were a lot of great ideas in this chapter, so hopefully you and your recollections are fired up!

Add your answer to start Your Own Story as to how and why you became a teacher to question 1 in chapter 15, at the back of the printed book. Also, you can visit the Teacher Talk website or Facebook page.

-ZP

CHAPTER 2

Regrets? Have You Had a Few?

Now, that's a silly question. Of course, we all have regrets in life, but the real question is whether our choices negatively impacted our lives. How will we ever know?

Maybe I should have tried to become a lawyer, but I dreaded the thought of working with people who (allegedly) committed crimes. Also, my high school guidance counsellor—a man—said I wasn't the right material to be a lawyer. In those days, women had to fight hard to break into male-dominated professions. It just seemed easier to go into the teaching profession that welcomed everyone. I don't regret it one bit, as I loved working with people who wanted to learn, and teachers are the best colleagues.

—ZP

have no regrets at this time, but when I retired at fifty-six, it seemed a bit too young to do nothing, so I did some real estate, seven long-term occasional teaching jobs, worked in a winery, and ran a B&B for ten summers. As well, while teaching I did volunteer work at the Shaw Theatre and my local museum.

———

I wouldn't say I have regrets now, but I did want to supply teach and keep up with the young people and share my knowledge. However, it was difficult to get on the "list," since the rules had changed. I'm intelligent enough to understand that the demographics of young, unemployed teachers needed to be addressed. I was at the same point thirty-four years ago—forced to supply teach before getting a job that was out of my comfort zone.

Instead, it provided me with the opportunity of having a lot of time on my hands. So, I put myself on this direction of writing a book and was glad to learn about how to get published and learn about writing stories. In addition, this collaborative book kept me in contact with a lot of amazing teachers I had worked with.

After reading so many books and working in a library, it was both egotistical and ambitious to think I could add to the compendium of writing. But I also saw that lots of different books sold—novels, nonfiction, and story collections. So, I thought I might contribute something to this world of possibilities, given some good writing courses and guidance that I discovered was out there!

———

Absolutely no regrets. Retirement has been fabulous. I'm as busy as I've ever been and am involved in so many activities that give me pleasure. As many retired people say, "I don't know how to fit everything I want to do into the day."

———

Yes! I should have hung in for the money!

———

I never regretted leaving the job.

———

I thought I might be anxious about retirement, but I got into a daily routine, kept busy, and have a supportive family to negate any second thoughts. To date, I have had lots to do and am busy on a number of projects, so no regrets. I do miss the daily interactions, but I will adjust and make contacts to keep in the loop and maintain some amazing friendships acquired over the course of my teaching career.

———

No regrets whatsoever. I had a very full and fulfilling career, and now I am enjoying the fruits of my labor.

———

None—the first September after retirement, I applied for a part-time job in my town's parks-and-recreation department and have been enjoying meeting new people, staying active, and getting to know my community, while applying my skills and indulging my interests locally. By the way, I now work with seniors—I knew it was time!

———

I have no regrets about retiring, although it seemed a bit scary at first.

———

I regret that I have not kept up with all the new technology after I stopped working. I need to upgrade my computer skills that were good during my working days. I believe it's important to keep up with technology; new inventions ought to make our older years easier. Also, I'm waiting for self-driving cars to be perfected! As I get older, I fear losing my vision and perhaps my license to drive, and it will limit my ability to go almost everywhere, as I live in a rural area.

———

I regret I don't have a time machine to go back and talk to all the students I may have treated with less respect than they deserved. I still want to correct all the wrongs and perceived hurts, to explain and apologize if possible. I certainly made mistakes in my younger days. Today, I wouldn't send students to the office for infractions that I could have dealt with myself in this more mature iteration. Sometimes, the principal or VP decided on consequences like the strap back thirty years ago; it can always be handled without corporal punishment. I am so glad the strap is no longer permitted. I did handle discipline better as I gained experience and now wonder why it was even needed. But in lieu of a time machine, I would say "I'm sorry" to those I may have disciplined inappropriately.

———

Cliché time. I've been retired ten years. Never been busier. My wife and I downsized and moved to a wonderful place facing the Pacific Ocean. We have traveled more than we ever did while I worked. I am on the go all the time. I have enrolled in university and am taking courses of interest. We have new friends and keep in contact with many of our old friends. Because I am not working, I can say yes to many more activities. I no longer need to play politics with the staff or administration. I can also say no when I want, with little or no guilt. But mostly I say yes. It's better to say yes and try something new than to say no and never know the what-might-have-beens in life.

———

It's pretty much unanimous that all of these people loved teaching and do not regret retiring— unless they went too early to miss out on a decent pension. It's important to have enough in your pension plan, as it can be harder to gain employment as a senior citizen. Plan well and carefully. Now add your thoughts to question 2.

-ZP

CHAPTER 3

The Best Advice for a Successful Teaching Career

Far out, psychedelic, cool man, out of this world. This was my secret teen language. It was both hot and cool to be young in the sixties and seventies.

Now the language is harder to decode; when kids say things are sick, it means that's a good thing. *Lit* means it's really cool, fun, or exciting (I think). Therefore, the retirement stage is lit too.

I lost the ability to be cool way back when— but I connected with students in my own quiet way, and I hope it made a difference.
—ZP

- Treat each day as a new beginning, and be open to new challenges.
- Be a positive role model for all by being yourself, and find your comfort zone.
- Never assume you know all the answers, even if you think you do.
- Expect the unexpected.
- Treat everyone as you would want to be treated.
- Be open to change, and accept criticism that is warranted.
- Always be willing to go the extra mile for staff and students.
- There is no such thing as a dumb or stupid question.

bove all else, have fun.

To have a great teaching career, one must like the students; enjoy their enthusiasm, strengths, and weaknesses; and rejoice in their achievements. Remember, how far they have come is the important thing.

A couple of things certainly come to mind. First and foremost, don't allow yourself to get burned out or in a rut. That involves knowing yourself and being proactive in maintaining your health.

For myself, I'm easily bored and need change and mental stimulation. Thus, I regularly took night and summer-school courses. Also, over my thirty-one-year teaching career, I constantly sought out new courses and subjects to teach. I also changed schools five times when new opportunities arose.

I took a year off to "recharge my batteries" after twenty years of teaching. I used the "four for five" plan that the board allowed and used that year to travel with my family, teach overseas, and start planning for life after retirement. It was one of the best decisions I ever made.

———

Teaching is not for everyone. Good teachers are few and far between. Students will get poor, average, and good teachers. At the end of a career, I believe a teacher actually learns as much as he or she has taught.

———

My best advice is as follows:

- Show your true self.
- Never be afraid to let your guard down.
- Emotion is good, even when you lose your cool.

———

The lovely, quiet fifteen-year-old girl in the class I'll call "R" had suffered a great personal tragedy. Her brother had died the day before in a terrible accident, and I imagine her parents didn't know where to send her, so she came to her classes in high school. I didn't know if she wanted to talk about it, as she had slid in quietly late to class and sat without any expression. I had just heard, but her classmates in grade ten were unaware of what burden she carried with her that day, so I tried to show her extra kindness. I told her that if she wanted to leave at any point, she could do so. But she was stoic and insisted that she would go on as normal, since that's what her parents wanted.

The class lesson was completed, and I organized a trivia game for the last ten minutes of our eighty-minute-long class. While we were playing a word game at the end of class, I asked if "R" wanted to keep score at the blackboard. Good thing she did. She was such a brave person to participate, and to my horror, five minutes before dismissal at the end of the day, her world came to a stop. The afternoon dismissal announcements came on not with the regular housekeeping information about late buses but about her tragic loss. How devastating it was to hear the principal's voice coming from the public address to say he had sad news to announce to students and staff. I couldn't believe it. I can't imagine what went through the sister's mind at that time. Luckily, she could face the blackboard to hide her emotions away from the other students in the class, many of whom weren't aware and were asking inappropriately, is that this girl? Is it this girl here, "R" and her brother? Although the principal made a heartfelt announcement that her brother had died, I'm sure he was unaware that his sister was listening to this news in class. Even worse, several of my students had no clue that his sister was standing next to me, hiding her face and the pain in her heart by looking at the blackboard. I successfully gestured not to ask, and we would all leave quietly and speak personally to her one on one. That day was a huge reminder that life is more important than teaching the lessons. It's about caring for and about each person, each student as an individual and part of our lives. My best advice is to try to know what is in the child's heart as best you can.

———

Be friends with the main secretary.

———

Change with the times. If a new curriculum unit comes up, try to see the positive in this approach. Also, upgrade your teaching credentials. I added more specialty areas like history specialist and law, as well as librarianship parts one, two, and three during the course of my career. It used to be so hard in the early days; you had serious-looking librarian ladies keeping you at a teaching course late on a Tuesday night to fulfill the hours of instruction. It was so hard when you had to get up and work the next day and children were at home probably waiting to have their bath and get a snack. In addition, you usually left school and ate on the run, drove to the city, and paid exorbitant parking rates.

I had one professor who had posted the hours of the additional qualification course publicly survey the class to change it from Tuesday and Thursday and speed it up by adding a couple of Saturday whole-day sessions. The people in my class voted for it! And the reason for this change was that the professor wanted to go to swim lessons.

Now these courses are so much easier with online courses. In this instance, it is an improvement if some of the work can be done on the computer on your own time. I really enjoyed the

Guidance Part 1 class that let me log in to a discussion group from my home in the evenings for a couple of hours.

———

Be consistent with your treatment of the kids in your class. Attempt to get along with all the staff.

———

Get involved in extracurricular activities and committees to really know students and staff. I learned after a few years that these connections were the most memorable. At first, I thought the lesson plans were most important. I was pretty uptight, but luckily some good friends of mine let me learn the things that were really important in teaching as in life.

I finally understood that after many years of working with people—but of course, after I had made several errors in judgment—I wish I could go back in time to redo stuff I said in haste.

———

Keep learning, especially from your students. Don't be afraid to say "I don't know," but be sure to find out before the next class!

———

The best advice is not to give advice if it's not asked for.

———

My best advice would be to follow your heart and know that this is something you love! An observation after the fact is that one must love children, understand children, have been around children, etc. Most of all, for me, as an only child, I believe *having* children makes one a better teacher.

———

Find new challenges to keep from stagnating as a teacher. Whether it be professional development, choosing new courses to teach, getting involved in interesting extracurricular activities, or some other new experience, avoid getting into a routine.

If you find your work exciting and interesting, chances are that it will rub off on the students.

I'm a firm believer in in-school professional development and also regularly took courses at night school and summer school.

Toward the end of my career, I realized that I was getting bored with teaching and took the rather extreme step of taking a year off. Our school board allowed me to take a four-for-five-year plan (accept 80 percent of my salary over the five years), which lessened the financial burden of my absence. It was a wonderful decision, and I returned to the classroom reinvigorated.

———

Be open to change.

———

You should have a passion for what you do. Working with students is demanding work, without any readily apparent rewards—but if you really connect with kids, it is the most satisfying profession. Nothing was more rewarding than seeing that a kid was having a "eureka" experience.

———

Observe and learn from the best teachers around you, if they will share. Ask your students at the end of the course; survey them.

———

Work with people you like. Find a school and a department where you feel comfortable.

———

My advice to any and all is to find something to do that you love and do it. If you do not love teaching, then please, for the students' sakes and your own, get out of teaching. I have seen too many young teachers go through the motions; consequently, I have seen far too many students suffocate because of a lazy, un-motivated, uncaring, or uninvolved teacher. Get out of teaching if you don't love it. Please!

———

It's important in a career, when you meet so many people, to stay positive. I met thousands of students and, of course, parents—although the parents seemed to get so much younger as I neared retirement. Also, there were many interactions with administrators and coworkers that included custodial staff and board executives, and it was important for me to get along and do a good job.

Secondly, mark special occasions with a card or a small gift—for me, giving at Christmas was important and established a personal connection with people that has lasted my whole life.

———

It is still sometimes hard to convince other nonteachers that 3:30 p.m. is not the end of a teacher's workday. For most teachers, it is the start of extracurricular sports and clubs that add so much to the students' experience as well as our own. I always found an after-school interest-tennis, debate club, sports, clubs, and providing a spot for students to read and study in the library after school were among the best of times. Please share your advice to teachers for a successful teaching career to question 3.

-ZP

CHAPTER 4

The Greatest Days in Teaching

No, the greatest days teachers remember are not going on their summer vacation, despite what you have heard. *I think the greatest days include all the connections we make with the young people and coworkers.*

I'll say no more, since there is so much here about the best times in teaching and my colleagues have provided their best stories.
—ZP

———

The best news for me always warmed my heart. I enjoyed being told by the children that they wanted to be in my class. Also, it was rewarding to hear heartfelt gratitude from parents on seeing the progress their child made in their time in my class.

———

There are so many "best days" of teaching—the first day of every school year, when you meet the new students all looking eager and happy to meet you and find out about you. The last day of school before summer, when you have seen them mature and know each student as an individual and that they have learned from you and grown as people.

Christmas was always special, as students often gave you unexpected cards and gifts. I always tried to provide some treats for my students. Food played a big role in our connections. And yes, we even had parties. Students never objected to candy canes and chocolates on special occasions, including Easter, Halloween, and Valentine's Day.

The last day of school is also special; as a teacher, I had seen them grow up and knew what they had accomplished. Graduation days, when you see the students come back for their diplomas and you hear what plans they have in their future and their road to success somehow involved you, are especially rewarding. To know they are on their way to a successful life—and I played a part in that life. I loved giving awards for top student in history, knowing that little bit of money would assist them to buy books. Also, library awards I presented were special, as these students really enjoyed reading and held a special bond with me. Most of these students came daily to see me, and we enjoyed talking.

———

I guess one of the best days was when my teacher buddy and mentor Brian and I took students on a field trip to the Royal Ontario Museum. We had a wonderful tour of the medieval area, and then we broke for lunch with clear instructions on when to meet back for the school bus back to Brampton. To our surprise, two boys missed the bus going back to the school. I was really freaking out about what I would have to tell the parents—that I had lost them. In the days before cell phones and Internet, we had no way of knowing where they were. Brian assured me everything would be OK. I dreaded the phone call home to the parents and was shocked and surprised to hear the "lost" student pick up the phone at home when I told him I was calling to speak to his parents. Apparently, they hopped on the subway and found the bus home to Brampton, because they had taken off to the Eaton Centre for lunch and had even beaten the school bus home! It was a great relief to know they were home safe. And students wonder why we are so adamant on field trips that everyone pays attention to the time and place of meeting to go back. It's a teacher's nightmare to be missing students on the way back.

—•—

No special best day. The happiest times of teaching were in my first years at an academic high school.

—•—

There were many best days of teaching. In my first year, the students put together a very successful newspaper. On a trip to Washington, the hotel manager said, "Bring back these Canadian kids!" for they were the best behaved he had ever experienced. In later years, the students put together a very successful history conference for the whole board.

—•—

I've thought of this question often over the past number of weeks and had hoped that a specific memory would surface, but I'm unable to think of a specific day. I enjoyed my teaching career, and there were many happy moments, but none that I'd call the best.

On a general level, the days that I found the most satisfying were those when I had a student with low self-esteem experience an activity that he or she completed successfully and was pleased with that success.

———

The auditorium filled with students and teachers singing the national anthem. Powerful.

———

Way too many to recount or remember but here are a few:

- Having kids celebrate your accomplishments like a birthday or the birth of your children
- Getting a standing ovation in class for trying my hand at something technological—new beginnings
- Having students confide in you about their fears and dreams
- Lots of fireside chats after school, with many students who shared a lot of themselves and their concerns and issues of the day
- The first day of the school year and the first day of my teaching career

- Getting unexpected thanks from those you least expect it from
- Coaching—nothing better than seeing kids excel or reach a goal
- Being asked for a reference
- Doing vectors with a group of grade-ten applied students using a map—totally awesome day—made me realize even though I knew it that kids of all abilities are capable of so much more
- Last but not least was the visit last year from a student who graduated ten years ago who heard I was retiring and came in to thank me for keeping her grounded and helping her achieve her goals of going to and completing her college diploma, despite the hardships she has endured; she remembers me telling her that life has a way of taking a long time for things to happen—stay the course

I was fortunate to have many, many good days. I would characterize good days as those that had everyone, including me, totally involved in what we were studying.

Best day, during a festival of Canadian films, an audience of grades nine to twelve sang the national anthem, joining in with the movie they were watching. They felt very connected and inspired by the film as a multicultural crowd; it was very rewarding to see them all connect to the story, Canada, and each other.

There were many, many. On an everyday note, it would be the fact that as you walked down the hall or the students entered the classroom, you would make eye contact. It was great. It was like we are in for a treat today, together. Let's get to it.

My last day of teaching was one to remember. My homeroom organized a grand celebration. The students organized food, cards, former students, even a visit, and a thank-you from our local member of Parliament, who was a friend of one student's family. Ego aside, I knew I had made the right career choice, and I knew that in some tiny way, I had made a positive difference in some people's lives. In the school where I taught were five former students of mine who were now teachers. In the board I worked for, over twenty former students. In other boards, I don't really know.

———

It may be the hardest question-what was your best day of teaching? There are so many answers possible! Please add your best day to the website, FB page, or in print in chapter 15.

-ZP

CHAPTER 5

The Nightmares or Worst Days of Teaching

The worst day could just be the last straw.

It may be nothing horrible, just a random series of events. It could be that you didn't sleep well, and the copier didn't work, so your lesson wasn't ready, and the projector wasn't working or a returned test led to students arguing with you about their marks.

Sometimes it's a terrible blow-up or meltdown. Shocked that the police were called to the school because a student brought a gun to school? Did anyone know if it was a toy or real? Hopefully, we are able to cope with these crazy situations that affect us even long after we have retired.
—ZP

I can't recall if it was the second or the third day after the 9/11 attacks, but it was definitely my worst day of teaching. The high school I was working at had the highest number of Arab students in the district, and the news media was full of anti-Arab stories. There was so much outrageous rumor, fear-mongering, and distortion of the tragedy. When I looked at so many of my Middle Eastern students, I could see the confusion and pain they were going through. I could easily imagine what some students were saying to them and about them. As a teacher, it was a day of helplessness, sorrow, some fear, and even some anger.

———

Probably when I swore at my principal because she said she no longer wanted the results of a project she had asked me to do.

———

I would say there are several, but the worst of all was in my first full-time job. I was teaching French, geography, and art to grades six, seven, and eight. My inexperience and some strange circumstances led to a boy getting the strap. The boy was very hurt and angry. It has impressed me deeply, and I vowed never to see that happen again to a person I taught. I only wish I could have apologized, then and even now. Luckily, the strap was banned after that year.

———

The day I witnessed one of my students having an epileptic sei-zure. No one knew that she was epileptic, so we were in a panic. I have never felt so helpless.

———

The worst days were during the strike action.

———

Another side to teaching is the mandatory staff meetings. Often new initiatives were presented at the end of a workday, when we were tired. I suppose it happens in all professions, and we need to keep up with changes happening with light-ning speed.

———

I sent a student to the office, but they sent him back within a couple of minutes. The class just laughed. Apparently, the admin staff was all in meetings. So now what?

———

Bad days occur all the time, but I remember one class that made my semester twelve years ago a living nightmare—each day a new crisis and moment.

I think they took great delight in making me fret; funny that I still see some of them, and they are the first to say *sorry* for that semester and wonder how I held it all together despite the immaturity and ongoing disputes—go figure!

———

Despite all the different strategies we have for teaching language skills—not being able to reach a student is frustrating for both teacher and child. I always cared about each student regardless of their ability. It pained me when I couldn't help them learn and move forward.

———

It seems likely that I would teach history in high school, and all my practice teaching was aimed at that level. I did not have much experience with younger students and didn't even take French as a Second Language Part 1 teaching certificate in teacher's college at Faculty of Education University of Toronto.

The hiring of teachers is in conjunction with baby-boom cycles. So, when there are lots of kids, teachers get hired. But when there is a lull—and it comes regularly (boom and bust)—teachers get laid off from work. Unfortunately, when I graduated from teaching, we were in just such a bust cycle; it was a difficult time in 1979 and 1980 to get a job, since there was a surplus of teachers, and many with seven years of experience were getting laid off.

The few job openings were for the booming junior level and French on Rotary. I got a job up in a small town. It was a great opportunity to build my résumé up with real experience. I tried hard but didn't realize and was shocked to learn some parents actually didn't want their children to learn French.

Looking back, I realize how nice that boy was who refused to answer me in class. He knew his parents would be angry with him, but he never caused me trouble. I figured it out on parents' night, when his parents told me so directly.

———

It's the in-between stuff that's hardest. When a student confronts you, and you know it's right or wrong, that's easy.

———

The only really bad day of teaching I can recall was when a boy in my chemistry class left the room and ended up in a fight outside the class, due to an ongoing dispute with another boy over a girl. In attempting to break it up, I got thrown around quite a bit, as well as verbally abused by the student, who I believed was a decent lot. Tempers have a way of bringing out the worst in us. It shook me up quite a bit and resulted in me being sent home for the day. We resolved the issues after a week or so.

———

After rereading all of these stories, I'm
starting to feel better about my bad days;

they don't seem as bad in hindsight! By writing them down and sharing with you, I have been able to release them from my nightmares.

-ZP

CHAPTER 6

Tips for Surviving Teaching in the First Few Years

At those times when students are barely paying attention, try to figure out why. It may be something outside of your control. On those days when you know why you cannot capture their attention, find your happy place, change your expectations, and realize that when it's the morning after Halloween, it wasn't your lesson that was the problem.

Everyone has work problems, and some can be much more difficult than inattentive children. We all had to figure out what to do when things weren't going to plan, and think on the spot when an unusual emergency situation arose.

Seeing a student in an epileptic seizure for the first time caught me fully by surprise. Luckily, that student and I had a lot of help near at hand.

**Go with the flow and change
direction if need be.
—ZP**

——

I actually found the first year of teaching quite easy, since I got lots of help from my department head and other teachers. I listened to the advice of the successful ones and tried to avoid the jaded and negative ones. Most of all, I tried to keep a sense of humor and not take myself too seriously.

——

All jobs have stress in one form or other. Have a stress-release activity built into your regular routine. For me, it was sports. In the winter, I played recreational hockey twice a week. One of those weekly sessions was with other teachers, and it was often the perfect opportunity to blow off steam. In the spring and summer, it was tennis a couple of times a week that filled that role.

——

Ask lots of questions to figure out where your students are and what your coworkers are doing. Make your students feel good and successful even for trying. Many students are late bloomers and just not ready for the level of material that you have now.

——

Listen to the kids to find out if they have a quiet place to work at home, or are they expected to babysit siblings or do chores when they come home?

I was surprised when I visited the home of a young student who should have been doing well in French in grade seven, as he had French-Canadian background. However, when I got to his home, the mother had a group of children, as she ran a home daycare. The place was full of fun, noise, and bedlam; snacks; and toys, but it was not a quiet place for the student to do his homework. So, I learned a thing or two about jumping to conclusions, since you need to walk a mile in your students' shoes to know what they face at home and outside of the school walls.

———

Advice #1—Tomorrow is a new day; leave it at the door when you leave.

Advice #2—Leave time for you each and every day. The stress of the job is daunting; you need time to relax and unwind.

I have been a pretty even-keeled person throughout my career, so the same rules apply as they did at the beginning. Remain positive, finish the job, and relish your accomplishments; too many people mail it in too early, and the learning and teaching suffer, so don't look past the end of your nose. The end will come soon enough.

———

Be prepared to do a lot of hard work and stick with what you know works. Believe in what and how you are presenting concepts—easier said than done. I realize a lot has changed. In my day, we were told *how* to teach—not why—even if it didn't produce results, especially in methods of reading at the primary level. The primary supervisor was to be feared! Years later, I was approached and asked for an outline of a phonics method I used (until it was banned). It's funny how things go full circle.

———

Lectures and teacher-directed lessons sometimes lead to students being bored, if not interactive enough. Some students work better one on one. Group work excites some young people and upsets others, who feel the workload isn't fairly distributed. Others are visual or auditory learners. Unfortunately, they often don't know themselves how to learn best or how to study. Learners are more likely to be engaged if there is an emotional connection with the teacher; kind words of encouragement are best.

———

Students can have it really rough at home, and we are often totally unaware. One girl shared a bedroom with five sisters. Another girl shared a bedroom with her mother, and Dad slept on the sofa in their tiny basement apartment. They all wanted a better future. She was bright and hardworking, so I tried to do what I could to help her in the school library and provided references in future schooling and jobs.

———

Work hard and study the curriculum. Be nice to the students, co-workers, and everyone. Remember, you are on a team to prepare students for their lives and are often their role model.

Everyone is focused on making sure the lesson's facts are taught. But after experience, we realize it's the people and the relationships and caring about one another as people that makes a difference. The kids remember how you treated them, not exactly what you taught. I learned this after students saw me after graduating. I was a history teacher, but it was integrated with English; at first, I thought that was why they always said, "Hi, Miss _____. You taught me English at high school," but later on I realized it didn't matter, because they enjoyed my class.

———

Make your classroom a welcoming place they want to come to. Don't punish kids with harsh tests or assignments to prove a point or make you the hardest, toughest SOB on staff. It's not about the facts or being right.

———

Life is too short for making people feel bad about themselves. So, our job as teachers is to help each student be successful.

Be nice to your principal and department head, and, may I add, everyone you work with. It never hurts to have friends and people who like you. You gather more flies with honey than vinegar.

After you retire, you will likely see few people from your working days, as we all tend to move in other directions after the work finishes.

———

Don't volunteer for too many activities.

———

The principal can make your life wonderful or difficult. I was always able to get along with them. As a department head, I found that sometimes communication in a big staff is difficult, and leadership was not my natural trait, but it can be learned. Listen to your staff and ask for their help and advice. Also, admit it and apologize when you make mistakes.

———

Walk outside on lunch and breaks—near trees and nature if possible—to clear your head and refresh yourself. Taking care of yourself is another way to bring back your best self to the classroom and other people.

———

Find a mentor as soon as you can. I was very lucky to have two teachers who generously helped me get through my first year. Plan to teach many different levels, in terms of ability and age, so that you expand your understanding of how kids learn.

———

To survive teaching in the first few years and to get to retirement age, you need to persevere and keep your sense of humor.

———

What many of these situations have in common is a mentor or colleague who is willing and helpful in teaching the newer teacher the ropes and how to negotiate the problems they may have already encountered. Life is an individual journey, but we sometimes get to the same fork in the road another person has already encountered. Helping one another and seeing other points of view were key elements when things turned out well. Add your thoughts to question 6 on the website, FB, or chapter 15.

-ZP

CHAPTER 7

Look into the Crystal Ball– Ways to Avoid Career Pitfalls

Completing a lifetime career and reaching retirement age alive make you a winner already! But many of our colleagues didn't make it or changed careers. Please don't skip this chapter, because how we got there is a unique journey. We have friends, family, and of course the students who energize us every day; they all travel near our hearts and minds without physically being in the room with us. As teachers, we want to acknowledge their impact on us. Read about more career stories contributed by twelve talented teachers below.

—ZP

Three rules:

- Try to get along with everyone, especially your coworkers.
- Be nice to your principal.
- Avoid gossip (which is rampant).

———

Be a team player, and don't get jaded when you are older and see the same program come around again in a new format. Phonics? In. Then out for twenty years. Next, include phonics as part of literacy program. Also, try to deal reasonably with people who support us—either through their computer skills or providing the physical space we teach in. It's communication of your needs to others that will get the job done right!

Keep active, and have fun with the students, because that is why you got into teaching. Get involved with clubs and teams and extracurriculars; those students will come back and remember you. Be a mentor to students, but not their best friend. Keep a professional distance from your students on social media.

———

Remember why you chose this career—if it was to educate, then do that; if it was for the security, remember to be pleasant to the boss.

———

Love your job or get out. Forget retirement if you are not happy in teaching.

———

Enjoy your job! Sounds simple and sounds easy, but for me that meant making constant changes. I get bored easily, so teaching the same courses and the same topics and following the same lesson plans and the same teaching strategies were never options.

The way for me to enjoy teaching was to constantly try new things. I took advantage of any PD (professional development) activities I could, in some cases working with groups to put on these activities. Also, I took numerous night and summer-school courses that allowed me to teach new courses.

Lastly, I changed schools four times during my career, each time because of an exciting opportunity that presented itself.

———

Keep your sense of humor and pay attention to your health. Teaching requires a great deal of energy, so it is good to remain healthy.

———

Don't let teaching drive you to heavy drinking! I'll never forget in my first year of teaching over thirty-four years ago, as a young twenty-something, going out for Friday lunch with a small group of staff who were kind to me. I did not fit in with them. But they befriended me, and I'm grateful for this. Almost everyone in my elementary teachers' group ordered fish and chips, and some ordered a beer with it. We had forty minutes to eat and get back to school. I was surprised when one teacher ordered *two beers* with lunch, downed them, and said that it was unlucky to drink in odd numbers.

———

I couldn't have said it any better. Life gets so much better with a laugh now and again! While gossip is generally bad, getting to know your students and coworkers will enrich your life. My friend Donna and I once remarked that our library technician, Lynne, was a "human Facebook." She could recount from memory the whole family history of many people in a colorful and imaginative way, and she would tell them all about us too. So, when I got the chance to meet them, I felt as if they were already old friends. What a magnificent ability she possessed to tell stories. She did this because she truly adored these people. Now, add your story to provide career advice to others.

-ZP

CHAPTER 8

Financial Advice for Young (and Older) Teachers

Finances can be a funny thing. We never know enough when we are young, and no one can truly guess the future. Sometimes, one bad decision coupled with one incident of very bad luck can throw you into a financial tailspin. I've known people who worked hard and were cautious with money, but a serious illness, accident, or fire put them into bankruptcy. Others profited from a cheap piece of land they bought or came into an inheritance that allowed them peace of mind. A big family can be a true blessing, but the costs of raising children keep increasing.

Money, or making a huge salary, never entered into my mind when I was deciding to become a teacher. I heard stories of how in much older times teachers chopped wood for their hot

stove in the back of a small wooden one-room schoolhouse. I read the novels about pioneer teachers dealing with eight grades of students in one room. Teachers struggled hard, and in rural areas, farmers paid the local teachers with produce and eggs. Teaching didn't seem glamorous or a path to big riches but a calling.

Luckily, other teachers in the middle of the last century had organized and formed a union that allowed them to live with a good salary, benefits, and pension. I was the lucky beneficiary of the courageous actions of men and women who taught before me.

—ZP

Y ou don't always get something for free. Remember, "free" is a four-letter word.

Get additional teaching qualifications when you can; it's a financial investment in your future, in case you teach an optional subject or for some reason your specialty area is taken from you because of a new principal or department head. It's best to have some options. I had library and guidance options, in case I needed a change. They say a change is as good as a rest. As you get older, these additional teaching subjects will allow you to pro-long your career. Do it as soon as you can.

———

Start planning early, keep reevaluating progress, and stick to the plan as much as possible. This is easy to say but hard to do.

———

If you can, try to get to your full pension or what we called "the ninety factor," where your age and years of teaching add up to ninety. If you are pretty secure financially with other reliable in-vestments, of course you can retire at any time, but there are many years ahead, and finances can change.

If you are single, it will be harder to manage on one salary. That's why many people who are single or divorced keep supply teaching or find other tutoring jobs after they retire. Right now, it is very difficult for older teachers to get on the supply list, and the days are limited.

I did miss the benefits I enjoyed while working, so if your fam-ily is still young, health care might have to be purchased, as well as dental. This will cut into your overall income as well.

The teachers' credit union is also a great place for financial advice and getting a mortgage. Of course, you will need to get all the facts as to how much is government-guaranteed. I am sorry that I didn't understand or take advantage of getting a mortgage with the teachers' credit union when I was first buying a house.

———

Financial advice is a learned lifetime process, which many never get.

———

I should have started a saving plan other than what the school board had. If I had done that early in my career, I could have done all I did, but I would be more secure now.

———

Finances? It can be the luck or misfortune of history. Being born during the Second World War or the Black Plague was not a financially sound decision. However, many in today's demographic were lucky in the sense that we had the stability of having one employer or two during our whole careers. A good pension and job security allow you to plan ahead and invest in property or add savings. My advice would be to invest in buying a home (house or condo), for it provides you with inflation protection. As a young person with little credit, a bank will lend you hundreds and thousands of dollars for a house. Usually, houses hold their value and increase over time. Also, you can sell it as a last resort when money is needed.

———

Make sure you use all the tax-savings instruments the government allows. Be careful with investments in retirement savings, for you may make more money during your retirement.

If you find a tax-free savings account that is recommended, try to put money in on a regular basis. It's a way to save by paying yourself first. Automatic deductions from your paycheck, so you don't spend that money, are the way to go. It's great tool for younger people and anybody. Also, look into education savings plans for your children. They can be helpful but may be counted as income to the recipient at a later date. Be aware that it may impact their ability to get government funding like student assistance.

Invest wisely in the market what you can afford to lose. Take it slowly, as opposed to making rash investments to make the big money immediately. Remember, the market has lows as well as highs. Don't overextend yourself; live well within your means. Credit card debt can be the worst, yet credit cards used wisely can be a great boon.

———

For anyone who can afford it, find a reputable financial advisor.

———

Save for tomorrow and save for now at the same time. For example, take the trip you want to go on, as it may never come your way again. But most importantly, live within your means. Don't always look ten years down the road. With regular pay/grid in-creases, there is also the increase in all the other costs in life.

Try to reach the highest levels of accreditation so that you can earn the most money.

Enjoy the job. Keep your perspective. Take breaks when you can. Spend time with positive people. Don't be afraid to ask for help. Don't spend every cent you earn.

Money can't buy you love, but it certainly can make it easier to live comfortably! Add your thoughts on money management to question 8.

-ZP

CHAPTER 9

Charming, Memorable, and Trying Students and Classes

Why is there a running shoe stuck in the ceiling tiles? The class laughed when I called out the student's name for attendance. "He's up there!" they said, and pointed to the running shoe in the ceiling. They all convulsed with laughter.

I didn't know what to do, but I figured he probably wasn't up there. However, I was the new teacher in this class, taking over for a recent retiree. I knew that this was my first test, and I needed to pass without losing my cool.

I'll never forget those first funny yet stressful moments when I kept asking, "Where is this missing boy?" Was he in the bathroom or in the hallway? The class laughed with each suggestion I made.

After twenty minutes, I had to send the daily attendance form to the office, so I told the class that if I couldn't see him, I had to mark him absent. They realized that this could not happen. After a few protests, I guess the boy heard that I was writing his name down as absent, even though his desk had books on it. Finally, the student emerged from a book cabinet in the back of the room. I felt relief to know he had just pulled a harmless— and pretty funny—prank. I bonded with the students over this, and we all had a laugh together. I imagine it must have been cramped for him to play this prank for so long. I couldn't punish him, as it was a very inventive trick and made my first day at Turner Secondary one of the most memorable of my life.
—ZP

I was fortunate to teach some very remarkable students who have gone on to contribute their talents to make our country better. I feel confident that our future is in very good hands. Many have chosen professional careers; some are established writers, actors, doctors, lawyers, and best of all, teachers. Others are making sure that our houses are well built, that the electricity will work, and that even our parliament and provincial legislature have good representatives.

There were a number of special students, both good and bad. One reminded me not to lose my temper, and I am grateful to him. One who had Asperger's syndrome is now working on his PhD in English; we are on Facebook together. Another has just completed her career as a teacher, and I was at her retirement party.

———

We had whole-school assemblies where students sang or performed dances and plays, and the teachers showed their great spirit in joining in the performances. One of my students is now a famous country singer! He was always singing at our assemblies, and although I admired his voice, I never imagined he would become so successful.

———

In my first year, I taught grade three; I always read stories. I was reading *Little Red Riding Hood* (a less sanitized version than would be allowed now), and a little girl wet her pants because she didn't want to miss the end of the story.

———

My fondest memories include:

- A whipped-cream pie in the face to raise money
- A student sent out to get my keys out of a locked car who was back in less than five minutes with my keys and no damage to the car

- A school trip home from the Maritimes and each student with a live lobster as the parents picked them up at the airport
- A memorable assembly when the girl running for student council whipped out a condom and said her tenure would "give safety as well as a thrill"

———

I won't forget the young teenage boy who suffered terribly with a breathing problem. When there was quiet time, everyone could hear him breathing hard. I felt guilty to think how selfish I was to even consider it a hardship. He suffered all day and night with this difficult breathing. He was smart and managed to learn to live with his medical issues and was successful in spite of that. I marvel at how brave this boy and his family were in coping. You never know what others have to deal with at home. Often, I didn't appreciate how good I had it in my life until I saw what others had to deal with.

———

I remember some students who were bright and intelligent but didn't fit into the "box."

———

A girl in my grade-eleven ancient history class had a learning disability and worked hard to be successful. This was before there were many supports and legal basis for learning disabilities like

ADD or ADHD. We had a good relationship, but when a student teacher came in, she didn't realize that the girl needed extra attention. Luckily, it was a small class of twelve students. One day, the student teacher finished her lesson and had ignored this girl's question. Perhaps she didn't see her hand up; in any case, the girl caused a commotion and complained about everything the student teacher was doing. Her board note was unreadable, and she wasn't talking clearly enough. She was rude to the student teacher and ran out the door.

Afterward, the student teacher and I talked. She was angry with the girl and wanted to give her detention. I said that maybe she could try kindness first, because I saw the incident as a lack of communication. I also knew this girl needed more attention than the rest of the students.

The student teacher said this was unfair to the others in the class. But I knew that the others were mostly very secure boys, who were not even aware of any special treatment, as long as they felt things were fine for them. I had long realized that most students (and adults) are often so absorbed in themselves, they don't notice what is happening to the person sitting beside them. I don't think this is entirely bad. Perhaps it's just as well.

I suggested that fairness doesn't mean everything has to be exactly the same. I figured the student teacher might give the girl some special job or attention. Reluctantly, the student teacher agreed, and the next day she asked the girl to help out with the lights. She also gave her some special attention, asking her how she was feeling. It let the girl know she was noticed.

Well, you wouldn't believe the change in the student's attitude. She smiled with happiness and became super helpful that day. She offered to clean the board at the end of class. Then she stayed behind to tell the student teacher how much she enjoyed the lesson. The student teacher was ecstatic, as she felt she had made a real connection with the girl. I was happy too. It was a win-win, and the boys in the class hadn't even noticed what had occurred.

No one was more relieved than the student teacher, who learned one simple truth: you teach people, not subjects. Also, don't jump to conclusions about what students may be thinking. Sulking and anger may be a cry for help. Making the connection and figuring out how to reach individuals is important in this career.

———

Meeting a student many years later who remembered from kindergarten what I used to say about how it was important to treat a book with respect.

———

I have many fond memories. One day, I was heading to my class, ready to unlock the door. The students were crowding around the doorway and, let's say, just a bit too loud for comfort. I said, "Well, I guess I am going to have to whip you guys into shape." The next day, one of my boys said, "Here. You'll need this." Somewhere he had found a small leather whip fashioned like a cat-o'-nine tails. It was really meant as a keychain, which I used for years. I am grinning while I type this.

———

Some "bad" kids are just as memorable because they can be turned around with personal attention. I remember one boy was rumored to be smoking outside when he should have been in class. I left the class and went outside to the known "smoking hill" and located him. "Aha!" I called and gently got him by the ear while he threw down his cigarette. I pulled his ear gently (as in a cartoon) and told him he had to get into class. He played along, protesting loudly, crying "Ouch, ouch!" dramatically in order to entertain his friends. He came up to class with me, and we shared this joke as he acknowledged he was being a bad boy, skipping class. I didn't send him to the office, and there was no punishment—and he never skipped class again, as far as I remember. It was just old-fashioned personal attention, and sometimes that's all people want—to be noticed.

———

In a special class, one little girl only wanted to sit on my knee and touch my nylons!

———

A couple of the Down's syndrome kids were memorable because they were so happy and just wanted to be hugged!

———

Here's a very funny incident: I was engaged to be married in April of my first year of teaching. I was twenty years old, and some of my students were very near my age. The students in my grade-twelve math class were very interested in my upcoming wedding and began writing the number of days remaining on the board each day before I would arrive in class. They took a collection and bought me a wedding gift—a teapot with matching cream and sugar as well as a white negligee. One of the girls told me that they bought a white one because they thought a black one would be "too personal," and a red one would not go with my hair!

Needless to say, my face was very red when I opened that gift. Interestingly enough, I often see many of those students around our town, and we share fond memories of those early days.

———

I remember…

- I had a premier's son in my class.
- Also, I had a child whom I learned had later died from TB at an early age.
- I had a boy who cried to his mother because he was afraid he'd be in another class the next year.

———

A student who comes to mind was one who was in my grade-ten general-level class when I was teaching geography. He had a history of having moved around a lot, had been in numerous schools, and had a poor student history. In this particular class, I had a habit of giving surprise, short quizzes. This student got off to a very good start in the class, getting 100 percent on the quizzes, which I gave a couple of times a week. After a couple of months, he had one of the top marks in class at midterm, and he and I really connected. Unfortunately, the family had to move again. However, his mother called me and told me that his self-esteem was greatly improved, and he was sad to be leaving my class. I often wonder how his next school and life turned out.

———

I most remember the first kid who gave me a hard time. (Why me?) But the same kids who gave me a hard time often made me laugh. Also, the kids who had special talents or interests (e.g., athletes, jugglers, portrait drawers) and smart (or smartass) students are unforgettable.

———

Some of the male students thought it was OK to cheat, provided you didn't get caught.

———

The boy who came into library every lunch period to tell me about trains is crystal clear in my mind. He talked nonstop and didn't realize that his monologue put people off talking to him. He never took a breath or allowed you a word in edgewise. He was very kind and helpful otherwise. He needed to be taught how to read social cues, so I made it my mission to help him learn what pauses and questions would improve his listening skills. For months, we worked on how to talk to people, starting with greetings and allowing other people to say a few words.

Then he could respond but remember not to talk longer than a few sentences, to keep the conversation balanced. By the end of three months, we were having a conversation! He asked me questions after he said a few things. It was wonderful to see him become more sociable, and I saw he began to have more friends. He didn't need to spend his time talking at adults and hiding in the library at lunch, as he now had a friend his own age.

———

When I had some medical issues, I often had 5:00 a.m. hospital appointments. There was usually no issue with getting to school and starting period-one class at nine. One day, everything went haywire at the hospital and gridlock on the drive back to work. I was running a couple of hours late. This was in the days before cell phones, so I couldn't even phone the school that I was late. I was worried the grade-nine class had gone wild or worse, left the class to create havoc around the school. I was so wrong! They were the nicest bunch of kids ever.

When I arrived with barely five minutes to go in the class, the students were calmly sitting at their desks, talking or playing cards. My trusted attendance girl, Wendy, had taken attendance and filled out the absence slip correctly, and dutifully took the class attendance down to the office, just as if I was there.

———

Other exceptionally bright students showed promise in high school by running for student council. One of these students became a crown prosecutor, and all that I know of had successful careers. I hope all had happy lives.

———

One young lady loved history so much that she is now a graduate student in Aboriginal studies. I hope that somehow my history class helped spark this interest. She had come back often to the school to say hello. I had mattered and had influenced a young person's life, which is the main accomplishment for a teacher.

———

One student seemed to learn by osmosis. He would sit in my class and never take notes from my lectures or from the blackboard. He said he had it all "up here" in his head. I was very worried that he would fail, since he also never did his homework. However, he did very well on his tests and exams, scoring nearly perfect marks. He must have been some sort of genius before I realized what giftedness was or had encountered such people. I was very impressed but found it difficult to assess him.

———

There are so many memorable students! I think the story at the start of this chapter made me realize that laughter and poignant moments need to be shared-one event can remain in your thoughts for a lifetime.

I can imagine you having great memories
of special students, and I invite you to
record your special memories now.

-ZP

CHAPTER 10

Look Back on Those Funny and Fond Moments

It's a shame that many people do not realize how much they are truly appreciated, noticed, and loved until something dramatic happens in their lives. It would be an amazing world if we could celebrate each person in our lives every day and not have to wait until a birthday celebration.

The pressures of delivering the curriculum drive most workdays; however, each of us used the human touch as often as we could. I tried to help if a student in my class was having a bad day or time in life, but sometimes teenagers bottled it up and didn't want to confide their problems then or later that day. There were tests to take and lessons to teach. I truly hope these students had the support of good friends and family to carry them through.

I wish every student I ever taught the best of life, and I hope they know that each one is memorable because I got the opportunity to know them. Now read about the memorable students other teachers have taught.

—ZP

F ondest memory: the smell of the classroom!

I remember the president of our student council burning the team sweaters of the opposing school's football team in a garbage can in front of the whole student body!

I ought to have known, as student-council advisor, but I had no idea this was planned and had to apologize for the disrespect shown to our opposing (and local) football school rivals.

Anything can happen when the students get enthusiastic, but it certainly gave me a scare. Football was taken very seriously by my high school students, as well as the principal; that is an understatement. We were thrilled to get to the final championship game during the first year I taught there. The principal paid for buses so students from our school could go and support the team at the final game downtown. I'll never forget that principal, as he taught the whole school in an assembly a fabulous cheer that rolled like a wave of applause—up and down and loud and quiet. It was like he was playing a musical instrument with about eighteen hundred students. Fabulous.

———

The book-club reading program let me meet with more students interested in reading, and the book-giveaway days were fun.

———

Tense but fond moments were when the test results of grade two were coming in, to compare our classes with others in the province. One year, the result came in that they were a grade ahead already—reading equal to students in grade three and even better, in the fourth month of school—level 3.4. It felt wonderful, as I felt like I had passed with flying colors and my success was reflected in their success.

———

Changing jobs after an outbreak of meningitis was traumatic. I regret not letting students know earlier I was leaving, but the outbreak sent the students home for several days. In the meantime, I had found another position closer to home, and it would end an hour commute in each direction.

A grade-seven student lamented when I finally told them that I was leaving after the Christmas holiday, how sorry he was to find out so late, as "We wanted to throw you a good-bye party!"

He looked very disappointed. I did not realize that our connection was that close after only three months of teaching these students. People wanted to recognize me, and I didn't realize they needed to say good-bye. I won't make that mistake again.

———

It's always more complicated than you think it is. This became my motto, and I think it's not only true in school but everywhere!

———

My fondest moments revolve around classes that truly worked—times when the students were interested and engaged, rising to challenges, and really learning. I could step back and feel humbled by how well things fit together.

———

One of the great opportunities in teaching is the chance to meet a wide variety of fascinating, intuitive, and truly special people, and I speak of my fellow staff members. I quickly learned that by carefully selecting a group of people, I could create a world of experience and joy that could nourish and strengthen me. I remember the laughter in our prep room, the warmth of caring individuals, and their incredible kindness to me when I lost my father to cancer, and then, within the year, my mother to a stroke.

———

There were so many hardworking and keen students, and many went on to work in municipal government. I continued to see them after they graduated because my husband worked there too. It was always fun to recall the old stories with them as they now had an adult perspective.

Many places I went—baseball stadiums, bars, or just shopping in malls—resulted in frequent pleasant surprises, when I ran into a former student who still remembered me and reminded me of what I had taught! It's often a surprise as to what they remember and it usually makes me laugh.

———

An interesting angle to "regular" lectures and group work was the ability to try new teaching methods. One of these involved students becoming "experts" after fifteen minutes of reading about a topic. They then moved their desks into circles and taught one another their material. Lots of action and six people talking at once made it interesting, but I wonder how some students coped with the noise and how expert one can be in fifteen minutes. It was fun, and a change is always as good as a rest, they say.

———

One day in my upstairs classroom, I detected a foul smell like gas or oil. Some students smelled it too, but other teachers in the rooms beside me didn't have it. The office was not aware of any smell yet. Perhaps we were near a chemistry experiment across the hall. Because it was too much for me to continue, I took the class outside on the lawn for the balance of the period. Luckily it was a warm day. I believe in safety first when the students' health may be at issue.

———

History montages were all the rage a few years ago. A montage was a still life using humans as statues to depict an event; in my case, they were historical. I tried this one day to demonstrate the trench warfare in the battles of World War I. The students portrayed the soldiers in still life. They pretended they had weapons, were snipers, and did the famous scene of "going over the top" of the trench. Others were evading the rats. Some were throwing grenades, digging ditches, or dying. They did a great job, and it was very moving.

———

I loved teaching the notions of historical forces and differing philosophies of historical interpretation. I started with the ancient historians and then introduced spiral "repeating history" theorists like Arnold Toynbee and moved on to the economic historical basis of Marx and Engels. More modern theorists included the layer theory of historiography and proved fascinating to the students. They could look at events and people from other perspectives. I also enjoyed social history because it included more information about women than the traditional histories that concentrated on great leaders who were usually men. All this was an effort to teach them critical thinking rather than believing history was about memorizing facts. Art, science, or some measure of each? It was for them to think about and decide.

———

My first principal taught me that teaching necessitated learning about crowd control. A teacher needed to deal with group psychology, so never pit them against you. The teacher needs to learn how to deal with groups; otherwise, the students win, as there are more of them than you.

The method was to be organized and delegate jobs so that you are the supervising manager. One good way to manage the classroom was to have students hand out papers as you watch that they don't swat someone in the process. Also, it was very important to be fair and not have favorites.

———

Don't blame one student. Try to give general instructions so people won't be singled out. Instead of saying "Student X, stop talking," say to the whole group of children instead, "Everyone—listen up."

———

Memories of children in my arms are special. Also, I still receive Christmas cards and e-mails from many students. And yes, I have also attended the funerals of former students.

———

I have a respectful memory of parents whose son was in my history class in grade ten. Barely sixteen, the boy was ill, and I hadn't been aware until he was off having chemotherapy and not coming back to my class. He died of cancer later that year. Parents let the hearse drive slowly past the school, and the whole student body came out to pay their respects. I cried a great deal and was touched to know the parents cared that we needed to grieve as a school community; it was very kind of those parents to let us have that opportunity. It was the saddest day I can remember, and I will never forget it.

———

It's funny to hear, but a muscular, tall, male physical education teacher had scared the grade-one class when he asked them to stand in a line. There was crying and fear. Finally, a female teacher with lots of experience suggested he make it fun to line up. So, that is what he did. There were no more tears the next day, and a perfectly formed line of wiggling six-year-olds, when this large man said in a mouselike voice to "stand thin as a pin!"

Teaching history and French resulted in fantastic independent-study presentations of up to one hour. French skits were funny and very creative; it was a pleasure to see. I eventually had to limit history seminar presentations to twenty to thirty minutes, or it would take up over a month of class time.

———

Being in a library as a teacher-librarian reminded me of the power of books. We ran a reading program that allowed struggling readers to read at their own level. We bought whole sets of books that appealed to the older teen, but the covers did not reveal that the text was at a less challenging level. It was important to each student to accomplish something; this program gave them that opportunity. One grade-nine boy was proud to say that he had "never read a whole book before!" He was very proud to have finished a book and passed a computer quiz on it. And we were happy for him to have this new self-confidence that came from that achievement.

———

The young people keep the older teachers in the loop. I learned from the students who read manga books that these weird but loveable Japanese-style comic/art books were cool and interesting. How much fun it was to read the book from back to front; literature was really cool and probably put some new brain synapses into me.

———

A rather unusual scenario occurred years ago, before we became aware of terrorism. We were lucky to have a lovely lady as the school library technician, whose job in part was to check in books from the book return at the main desk. One day, she pulled out a mysterious object from the book return with wires attached to what looked like fake dynamite. She picked it up and took it to the teacher librarian. After their moment of shock in realizing it could possibly be a bomb, the library technician walked the contraption over to the far window of the school library—just in case it was real.

Of course, the library was cleared, and the police were notified. Luckily, it was just a fake piece of metal and tin with a timer and wires attached. It was an amazing sight to see a remote-controlled robot take away this fake bomb—as it was finally declared. But the investigation did not take long to find the grade-ten boy who was the culprit. Many students had seen him with it that morning in the library. Apparently, he wanted to play a trick on his buddy but was discovered, so he just threw it in the book-return slot. He was suspended, and after facing court charges, was given a youth sentence. I believe it was the same boy who had hidden in the ceiling on my first day.

We all marveled afterward at how calm and brave our library technician and head librarian had been in dealing with this nasty surprise. These were days before terrorism was more common, so they did not think it was a real bomb that might have exploded.

———

Some of the best days were hearing the excitement of students who were going on to what they dreamed of after high school. Whether it was a cooking course to become a master chef or university acceptances and scholarships, it was always great to hear the screeches of joy as they were accepted into a postsecondary program of their choice and were moving onward in life.

———

One of the most memorable lifelong connections involves the kindness and generosity of students over the years. Many came to volunteer their time to help me and other students. "Random acts of kindness" were done before it became popular. All of these people are unforgettable.

Now record your thoughts online or by pen and paper as you prefer.

-ZP

CHAPTER 11

How to Decide When to Retire

I think the day when a heavy clay model of the Great Pyramid fell on my head was one of the first days I seriously considered retiring. Of course, there were many trying times before, such as when a student threw himself headfirst into a classroom garbage can—but that was way too early for retirement, as it was only my third year on the job! Also, many more serious incidents, where fellow teachers were assaulted, or students or staff I admired passed away prematurely, also triggered these thoughts. When I was younger and more resilient, I knew retirement was financially far, far away.

The $6 million question is always (as in any job) when is the right time. So when is it "just right"?
—ZP

———

reached my ninety factor (age plus years worked) and then some and felt the time was right both financially with the girls having finished school and the mortgage paid off, to try some new things—be it coaching, volunteering, working part time, or having time for me before my wife retires in a few years.

———

Retire—when you're making more negative comments than positive, it's time to go!

———

I was getting to the point that I felt it was time to depart. Morning drives were getting tedious, and the routine was getting dull. It seemed to happen more frequently that I needed to tell sleepy students to stand up and not talk during the playing of the national anthem every morning. I was just getting tired of the disciplinary aspect of the job.

I started teaching in elementary school as a French-as-a-Second-Language teacher, and we even sang the anthem in French together. I loved to sing, and I felt the excitement had gone out of this important daily event.

The staff I had joined as a young teacher had mostly already retired too. I missed my friends, the fun I had in our classrooms, and my fellow teachers' valued opinions. Teaching methods kept changing, and it was second time around for some ideas with new titles. Also, the excellent reading program with computer quizzes was getting more expensive to maintain. It was exciting that students liked selecting their own books and said things like "I've never read a whole book before!" It made me proud to be a teacher-librarian and see them love learning.

———

I decided to retire because of three things: (1) I reached my "ninety factor" (now the "eighty-five factor" of age plus years teaching). This allowed me to get an unreduced pension. (2) I achieved all of my financial goals; for example, I paid off my mortgage. (3) I started to feel tired and less energetic.

———

I took over as department head during a very difficult time for our math department. We managed to become a cohesive group once again, but the stress was taking a toll on my health. In addition, my parents were requiring a lot of care, and teaching did not give me the flexibility I needed in order to attend to their needs. I decided to retire from teaching—a very difficult decision—in order to have the time for them.

———

I was not happy in the school I was in. There was no chance to move because library positions were few and far between; I lost out on a school I wanted to go to when someone was grandfathered in.

———

I decided to retire for a number of reasons:

- I was getting older and didn't have the energy I once had.
- There was a generous gratuity.
- There was a $10,000 bonus that was conditional on teaching when one reached the eighty-five factor, and I was already at the eighty-nine factor.
- My computer skills were not up to the new standards.
- The students in my later years seemed to have a sense of entitlement that was not present in the earlier years.

Most students I will miss greatly, as they were keen and helpful and super nice, but the odd one did not treat me with respect, perhaps because I had no sway over their marks. Not being a classroom teacher shows you how some students come to think they are entitled to talk as loudly as they wish in the library area, where others are trying to study. In their defense, they are young, and some are very self-centered. But when gently asked to respect the tone of this large classroom and its rules, the responses that were negative clung to my mind, giving me many sleepless nights and some anxious moments.

The lure of retirement, with sleeping in and not going out on icy cold roads in winter to work also played a part. Indeed, I had engaged my mind for those many years, especially using computer programs and researching in the library, but my health had suffered. I was occupied with family matters, being a "sandwich" generation. I had aging parents with illnesses who needed help, as well as a child still in school who enjoyed dance activities and other events. The stress meant that I did not take the time to exercise properly; however, I made it a priority in retirement to get back in shape. It is amazing how much you can improve your health when there is more time to focus on yourself.

———

I retired when my first child was born. Teaching was a job, not a vocation.

———

I can honestly say that with the exception of a handful of days, I thrived in my career as a teacher. I never wanted to be a department head or an administrator. I wanted to talk about, share, and explore English with my students and hopefully pass on my joy to them. The best time to retire is when you have lots of gas still in your tank. Why go on and on and on?

———

My decision was a combination of a couple of factors. Firstly, as much as I generally enjoyed my work as a teacher-librarian, I realized that certain areas of the job were becoming more and more unpleasant, such as the inappropriate use of cell phones in the library. At the same time, I was being pulled by the after-teaching plans I had been contemplating for a few years. I'd always wanted to work outside at a golf course where I could play more golf, be outdoors, and get paid while doing so. There were several golf courses very close to home, and I'd already had a couple of offers that included playing in my off-work hours for free.

In the background were a couple of more abstract thoughts I'd been having. Over the past few years, I'd known of friends and colleagues who had either developed illnesses that had prevented them from following their retirement dreams or had, in fact, died unexpectedly. Also, I remember one of my friends who had recently retired saying that he had calculated that if he lived to the age of seventy-five, he had a little over five thousand sunrises left to see, and he was going to enjoy every one of them.

I thought about these and other ideas (including the financial implications) for about six months, and after discussing them with my family, I made the decision.

———

I wanted time to do some of the things I've always wanted more time for. Could I write a book? I had been an avid reader all my life and could see that many types of books had been published, not all of them great literature or all that successful. I hoped for medium success at least. If I kept working, I wondered how I could do this, as my parents were getting sick and much older, needing more help.

———

When I retired in 2002, they were trying to get rid of the "old, dead wood." There was a monetary inducement as well. I continued to do long-term occasional teaching for a few more years. I weaned myself off the job.

———

A variety of factors contributed to my decision. My husband, a retired teacher, was urging me to call it quits, but I was still enjoying myself at the independent school I had moved to from the public board. Everything there was more manageable: class size was capped at twenty-two, team teaching was encouraged, administrators were extremely supportive of building a cross-curricular library-skills continuum, and budgets were generous. As head of library and teacher-librarian for middle and senior schools, I had the pleasure of working with keen, capable students from grades seven through twelve in a variety of research projects, and my favorite thing was book talking and readers advisory. So why did I retire? One August, I just knew I was starting my last year of teaching. A change of administration had changed the school's mood. Social media were dramatically changing the teaching/ learning landscape. I had created an amazing library program but would need an incredible amount of energy to keep up with all of the possibilities in information technology. I realized that I wanted to leave at the top of my game, and I did.

———

Everyone has a personal journey in life that cannot be replicated. Your experiences were yours alone and had unique attributes. Why did you decide to retire? If you are not yet retired, then what might make you retire?

-ZP

CHAPTER 12

The Best Age to Retire

The newspaper clipping above the photocopier stopped me in my tracks. A retired gym teacher had just completed a grueling race competition by running, swimming, and biking! I was thoroughly impressed that anyone over fifty could still be strong and athletic. My perceptions of retirement were more sedentary, with some golf, walking, and gardening as the most strenuous activities, apart from bingo and reading a book. For others, it seemed that racing through mud bogs, biking, and running were still possible at an older age. I am now retired and lift weights as a result of this inspiration. It's never too late to be active—it will improve your life in many ways. I'm learning not to close my mind to things I have never done just because I'm older now.

—ZP

What is the best age to retire? It depends on you and your circumstances. If you have plans and the money, I'd say go as early as possible. If you enjoy the profession, it is a great one, so go as long as you can.

———

Retire when you feel you can't contribute to the students' education.

———

The best time to retire is up to the individual teacher and based on one's own condition, plans, etc.

———

There is no best age, in my opinion. I worked for five years past my "due date" (eighty-five factor) because I was enjoying myself and wanted to help our youngest through university. There is also the financial benefit that every working year after achieving the eighty-five factor meant an extra hundred dollars per month on my pension! However, I don't encourage anyone to stay on, at any age, unless they are still loving it. The best advice, which I received from many, was, "You'll know when it's time"—and you do. I knew it wasn't time, and then it was!

———

Leave teaching when you still love to teach. Of course, get your years in for the pension, but then, why stay? You are not irreplaceable. The school will not put the flag at half-staff when you retire. If you have done your job well, some of your former students will want to be teachers too. So, get out of their way and let them teach. Better still, enjoy the fact that one may replace you and sit where you once did and teach in the same room where you once taught them. I taught at the same school for thirty years. Quite literally, I handed my classroom keys to a former student I had taught in that same room years ago.

———

I'm not sure what the right age is to retire, even though they talk lots about freedom at fifty. But fifty-seven to sixty seems like a good time to allow one to be able to do things while of sound mind and body, as age has a way of creeping up on you and may not be nice about it in some cases.

———

I don't think there is a particular age that suits everyone. It depends on so many factors—health, finances, etc.

———

The decision to retire is such a personal one. Perhaps one should retire when he or she doesn't have the stamina to be with young people.

———

Best age—before your "best before date"—no regrets at all.

———

I believe a person knows when the time is right. Whatever reasons—age, financial circumstances, etc.

———

The best age to retire from teaching is the age at which you no longer have the passion for it. I retired before that happened.

———

Passion and health, yes! Why work forever? Maybe age is just how old you feel. Go to the end of the book or our website/FB page and add your thoughts in question 12 on the best age to retire.

-ZP

CHAPTER 13

Do We Need a Bucket List?

I don't have an official list of things to do during retirement, but certainly writing this book is a priority. Once that's done, I'm sure there will be work to do to advertise and promote it. It's like a new baby, in that you want it to grow and flourish. It's surprising how a "simple" book project has changed in format since I first planned it and how much I learned about the process of writing and publishing. I hope that this proud collaboration of great minds and memories will be well received and that some of the stories you read here will help other teachers.

—ZP

———

I t is always a good idea to have some plans—whatever they are.

———

I don't have a bucket list. If you really want to do something, do it while you are still enthused.

———

My bucket list includes everything I enjoy doing and sharing time with people—family and friends. Of course, spending time with my husband is a huge priority, and we try to prioritize playing golf, going to the gym together, and having some nice meals. You never know when some illness or problem will prevent you from this quality time with the most important people in your life. My daughter barely needs my help anymore, as she has a full life of her own, but I appreciate seeing her grown up and capable, ready to take on the world.

———

My friend had a joke about the secret to a happy marriage and retirement.

The secret is going out.
He goes out Monday, Wednesday, and Friday.
She goes out Tuesday, Thursday, and Saturday.

———

My spouse and I enjoy travel, so we plan to see the Dominican Republic and Rome when the prices are not at their highest. This is one bonus of being able to travel in any month. Also, I heard September is a beautiful month.

———

If you and your spouse are both retired, I guess not getting into each other's space is important. However, having some activities in common with your spouse and other family members keeps you connected. Join a community group or club to contribute what you have the most of in retirement—your time.

Both of us are involved in the public-speaking club. Our local club is a very supportive group that has welcomed me, and I plan to continue my speaking at the club level. It's hard for a teacher not to have an audience anymore, so this should work out nicely.

———

I don't know if we need a bucket list, but it helps to have interests and hobbies. For example, I like to garden, power-walk, study online university courses, work around the house, and travel.

———

My bucket list includes enjoying good health. As a result, I work out at a gym three times a week. I also play a little social tennis and walk in nice weather. I try to have spinach smoothie drinks at least twice a week to improve the nutritional value of my diet. I am feeling stronger and am in better shape than I was in the last twenty years prior to retirement.

———

Don't always think of others before yourself.

———

The concept of a bucket list has been completely foreign to me. I've always lived a very active lifestyle and taken part in many different ventures. I played sports three times a week for most of my life. Most years, our family planned trips for the March break and summer months, so we always had those to look forward to. And I've always been heavily involved with volunteering both in student sports and clubs.

———

A bucket list is a fun idea—if necessary. Also, how about knowing yourself, doing what you love, and being happy! Forget other people's goals, ideas, and criticism. Just be yourself.

———

Whether you have an official list or not, you will find retirement to be a welcome rest with more control over your time. However, the bad news is that retirement has only freed me from one job. I still have all the other jobs: wife, mother, cook, laundrywoman, cleaning lady, and organizer of bills. Routine is good, as well as the freedom to pursue my interests. What's on your bucket list?

-ZP

CHAPTER 14

The Best Thing about Retirement

Whether it's sudden changes in our lives such as moving away or losing a close friend or relative, it is the people in our lives who come forward to comfort and help us. Without them, how could we negotiate the shock and feelings of great sadness on this rocky ocean of life? I have seen this happen over and over and wish we had a way to convey what we feel for others more often during our time together and not just when tragedy strikes.

Some days, if you feel blue or a student is out of sorts, you need those uplifting thoughtful actions or words. I was personally overwhelmed at how caring my fellow teachers were. One such occasion was when I was pregnant. My friends threw

me and another friend (who was also pregnant) a surprise baby shower. It was a touching and wonderful day in my life.
—ZP

———

The best thing is Argentine tango for those who like to dance.

———

The best thing about retirement to me is how time has become elastic. I can take as long a time, as short a time, no time, or all the time in the world to do a task, complete a book or project, or be out and about. Freedom from the clock is the greatest freedom of all. Often, it is only when my stomach growls that I realize there is a part of me that keeps its own internal time.

———

Do what you like—no roads off limits. Be free, and have fun when you can.

———

Tomorrow we are going to a sixties dance with friends. And yes, we will attempt to recreate a sixties wardrobe. The dance moves will be highly suspect and no doubt rather strange, but there will be smiles on our faces and memories in our minds. I don't have a curfew or an essay to write or mark the next day; there's that great elastic time again.

———

Now is the time for you and your family to get in shape, both in mind and body. When working/teaching, I was a slug physically. However, my mind was actively engaged and focused on my job. I had a lovely last few years in the school library that allowed me a lot of flexibility in terms of prepping orientations and lessons and teaching large groups. It was clearly not as physically demanding a job as my associates who taught physical education or demonstrated science labs with chemicals and equipment. It's surprising that there is a real stamina component to teaching music, French, English, or drama for hours on end. In history, there were some options to sit down once in a while, but in my retirement, I realized that I needed to get more active.

Luckily, it's never too late to join a gym, walk or swim, play golf and tennis, or take a dance class. I started to show up for my local gym classes and found out I really liked the weightlifting to music and aerobic dance classes. I could also do yoga, as long as I didn't do all the contortions or stretches with my short arms and legs. That really worked for me; also, the ladies I met were friendly, and I enjoy a new social group of friends.

For my brain workout, I decided to get creative and write a book, but I didn't know how. I leaned on my old friends, who fabulously helped me write this book with their stories and advice.

That's the best thing about retirement—you can do what you like, how you like.

— —

The best thing about retirement is not writing report cards and evaluating students. It was usually easy to give the As, but sometimes even those who got 97 percent came back to ask or complain where they missed those few extra marks. Having students fail themselves (which they did—although they accused me of failing them) for whatever reason was never a good part of the job. I always hoped that something good would come out of it, such as a realization that another path to follow, completing all assignments, or a better attendance record would lead to their success in the future.

— —

The best thing about retirement is not having long meetings to sit through, marking for hours on the weekends, and of course not having to do 120 report cards with three comments per student. Sometimes the student rarely attends, so it is hard to put in a proper comment. I didn't know the reason for the absences.

— —

The best thing about retirement is not having to go to work every day, through bad weather (any season), not to have to handle traffic, and being able to go away anytime of the year. I have nothing new to suggest to others, as I just carried on with hobbies and things I enjoy. Age definitely plays a role in what people do in retirement.

———

One great thing about retirement is enjoying restaurants and golf courses that are not crowded during weekdays. Tomorrow is a Thursday—I am meeting three fellow retired teachers for a late lunch (to avoid the crowd but get the lunch menu) after a workout session. Lunch is at a fabulous restaurant, talking over old times. *Tempus fugit* (time flies), but we enjoy it while we can.

———

Recommendation: I'm a serious proponent of "mindfulness" and wish I'd known about its benefits when I began my teaching career. A few years ago, I became aware of the concept when training to be a hospice volunteer. The tools it offers that allow a person to cope with life's inevitable obstacles are relatively easy to learn yet amazingly powerful.

———

Engage your mind. It helps to keep in touch with people on social media. On social media, I can easily keep in touch with what is going on in other people's lives. Connecting is easy without being intrusive or taking up other people's time or requiring several hours of driving. There are lots of good things about our modern world. Take the good, and work at improving the bad.

Get involved in causes, so our children and the next generation will inherit a good Earth.

———

Recommendation: It's never too late to get fitter. Walk in a mall, bike, lift weights, dance, do tai chi in the park, exercise to music, or get a treadmill at home. Do whatever you need to keep your body moving and fit. I recommend it, as people in the gym energize you and you feel motivated to come. I love the classes, but my husband likes the individual workout on treadmill and elliptical and weight training and spin or indoor biking classes to build his muscles. I am fitter now than I was at thirty years old; as a bonus, we get to learn what songs are popular with younger people, as most classes are set to music.

———

Do something! Don't just drink and vegetate. Don't miss out on fun with neighbors and friends. Keep your mind active as well as your body. Join a card-playing group, learn to paint, learn a new language, or just walk. The world will not beat a path to your door; you need to go out and seize the day.

———

I'd say volunteer at some level in your community. Life now provides you with the time to give back and leave the planet better for the next generation. There are ways to contribute to the environment by counting birds and managing weather stations, as well as helping out environmental groups with their fundraising and garage sales. Look into programs offered by your local public library that promote the crucial values of equality for all. Libraries are the hub of every community—with their books for reading and freedom-of-speech access through computers.

———

Be happy, and don't let the bad stuff get you down. Now you can grocery shop at off-peak times like Tuesday mornings! But on the bad side, this is a time when you start losing people like your parents and older relatives and friends. On the good side, it's easier to spend more time with them, and you can assist them in many ways—like driving them to doctor's appointments. Just be there for them as much as possible.

———

Take care of your teeth, and look for an affordable health and dental plan. Teachers' groups offer many retirees options through a variety of plans. As my father got older, he needed more care due to failing-memory issues. He forgot to brush his teeth. I found that the few teeth he kept were essential to his longer lifespan and the quality of food he received in the nursing home. Keep your teeth as long as you can.

———

It's a roller-coaster ride. What I recommend is that you keep moving forward and adapting to the new life. Moving forward is natural and often easy during a teaching lifetime, when the next steps are obvious. On retirement, you can't see the forest for the trees. A lot of introspection is needed to figure out what you really want to accomplish in this part of your life.

Now there are so many possibilities and hindrances—which all depend on your situation. Sometimes luck—good or bad—can play a big role. Combine that with a couple of bad or good decisions, and your life can be turned upside down.

———

Because I moved across the country after retirement, I have little opportunity to see many former staff members. Most I will never see again. Tennyson, in "Ulysses," wrote, "I am a part of all that I have met." I'm a lucky and rich person.

———

The best thing for me about retirement is that I have so many friends and so much support from truly caring people. They continue to keep in contact long after our working days are done. Human contact that teachers provide is never obsolete. The retired teachers who contributed their stories possess both intellectual and emotional intelligence, as well as a flair for writing. As a result, their personal, daily connection with their students and others is the key to their successful careers embedded in all of these stories.

I hope you enjoyed these stories about teachers and I trust this book lets you picture your endless summer of retirement.

Now you can add your thoughts on the best thing about retirement to question 14.

-ZP

CHAPTER 15

My Story: Add Your Story

Name

1. Why Did I Decide to Be a Teacher?

A. Education Autobiography

Schools Attended, Including Teachers' College, Date Graduated, and Teaching Subjects

B. First Training/Placements

C. Employment: Schools and Subjects Taught

D. Teams, Clubs, and Extracurricular Programs

E. Important Career Moves or Positions of Responsibility

2. Regrets

3. My Advice for a Successful Teaching Career

4. Memories of the Greatest Days I Had while Teaching Are

5. When I have Nightmares, I recall some of my Worst Days in Teaching.

6. My Favorite Tips for a Good Teaching Career Are

7. Looking in the Crystal Ball, Career Pitfalls to Avoid

8. Financial Advice for Teachers

9. Charming, Memorable, and Trying Students and Classes

10. My Funny and Fond Memories

11. Why or When to Retire

12. For Me, the Best Age to Retire Is

13. My Bucket List or Something Still to Accomplish

14. The Best Thing about Retirement

About the Author

A former teacher and department head, Z. Proudlock graduated from York University with degrees in French and history. She went on to study at the University of Toronto Faculty of Education.

Over the course of more than thirty-five years as an educator, Proudlock taught history, library science, law and French. She will never forget the many wonderful students and colleagues who enriched her life.

Add Your Story and questions at our website

http://teachertalkastorycollection-addyourstory.com

Facebook: Teacher Talk: A Story Collection

Made in the USA
Columbia, SC
06 April 2018